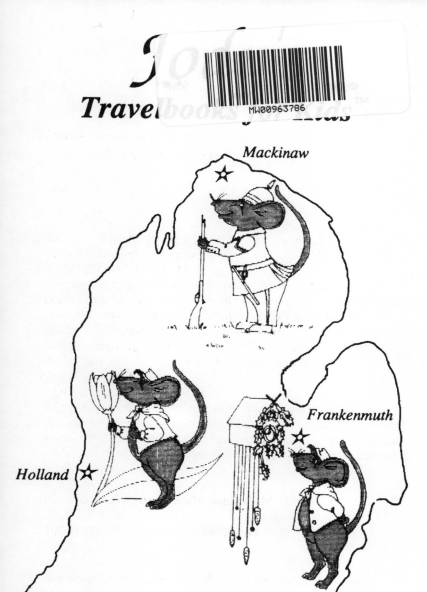

With special thanks to
the Michigan Chambers of Commerce.

Cover Picture: The Grand Hotel, Mackinac Island, Michigan.

Jody's Travelbooks for Kids™
Summary: Real-life travel activities for kids, framed by a story about an adventurous little girl and her big brother, who wants to grow up to be an historian. The series is named after Jody the Dutch mouse, who acts as tour guide.

Vol. III, Mackinaw, Michigan, is available from
Paint Creek Press, Ltd.
P.O. Box 80547, Rochester, MI 48308-0001

Printed and bound in the United States of America.

ISBN 0-9648564-9-2

This Whole Thing Started When . . .

my little sister, Katie Murphy, was almost five. Our family went to Holland, Michigan for the Tulip Festival that year. It was really fun until my sister turned it into a disaster.

Katie didn't know about travel diaries then. Two years later, her second-grade teacher told her class about the Italian explorer, Marco Polo. Marco became famous by writing about his trips to China. This inspired Katie to become a "famous tourist."

My name is Kevin, by the way. I love history. I know how to write, plus I'm old enough to use our father, Michael Murphy's laptop computer. Katie figured this would make me the perfect person to be her secretary.

I found out she was planning to give all the credit for our stories to a stupid stuffed mouse named Jody. That's when I told her she had to pay me. I don't work for nothing.

The Frankenmuth trip was the first one I keyboarded. Katie was seven. She liked the story, but not what I said about her. Oh well. After Frankenmuth, I wrote about Holland. That's where Jody the mouse joined our family.

It was a gloomy, wet November day. My mom made me and my little sister Katie change into warm clothes. Afterwards we sat by the fire.

One of the big logs let off a pretty shower of sparks. Our mother brought us hot chocolate and piping hot raisin bran muffins. My sister stared into the flames.

"Don't you wish we were back in the summer?" she sighed.

"Yeah, but I like this okay too," I answered, warming myself in the glow of the fire.

"Don't you wish we could go swimming in the Mackinac* Straits right now like we did last June?" Katie smiled thoughtfully.

"Brrrrrr!" I answered. The water in the Straits is only 50 degrees in June.

"I wish I were eating a piece of Mackinac Island fudge." My sister's eyes closed in pleasure. "I wish we were going clippity clop, clippity clop in a horse-drawn carriage," she murmured.

I shuddered at the mere thought of horses and Katie. You'll see why when you hear about this trip.

*Whether you spell it with an "-ac" (the French way) or an "-aw" (the English way), you still *say* "Mackin_aw_."

"Why don't you write about your trip to Mackinaw,* the way you did for Frankenmuth and Holland Michigan?" my mom suggested. She knew Katie was restless.

"Oh no," I said. "I'm the one who has to type it for her."

Katie jumped to her feet. "I'll need to have a long talk with Jody the mouse and Mich the turtle about this right away."

If you've read any of our other adventures, then you already know that Jody the Dutch mouse is a ratty rodent doll my sister got on our trip to Holland, Michigan. She takes Jody everywhere she goes. Mich the turtle is another stuffed toy from our trip to Mackinaw.

The Straits area is known as "The Land of the Great Turtle." Mackinac Island looks like the back of a turtle rising out of the water. "Mich," is Ojibway Indian for "great." Katie's turtle is fat. That's why "Mich" is the perfect name for him.

When you find out what really happened on this trip, you'll see how much trouble this dumb turtle caused.

---

*The name of the island and the Straits is spelled "Mackinac." The name of the area and the city on the mainland is spelled "Mackinaw."

"Now Jody and Mich," Katie said with great seriousness as she set the two toys down on the bedspread. "I need your advice."

"Why? Is there anything the matter? I'm always ready to help however I can," answered Jody, his eyes wide with alarm.

"Fire away!" cried the turtle, who had grown up around cannons and muskets.

"I want to write about our family's trip to Mackinaw last summer, but I can't remember everything. I need you two to remind me about what we did," Katie replied.

"Oh, that's easy," said Jody with a grin. "We rode in the van a lot."

"Well, you couldn't have done that on Mackinac Island," snapped the turtle. "No cars or vans are allowed there. And besides, you stopped in Mackinaw City. That's where you got me."

"How could I forget a thing like that?!" chuckled the mouse.

"Stop it!" cried Katie, covering her ears and frowning horribly. "Stop being mean to each other. You're not helping me at all!"

"As a matter of fact, it's all very clear to me," said Jody. "After your father bought Mich here, you decided to take him for a swim in the Straits. Your parents were upset. Your father wrung the turtle out. Your mother hung him up to dry in the van.

"Then we toured Fort Michilimackinac," said Mich. "Your brother Kevin loved it because it's so historic. It was built in 1715 as a fur-trading village and military outpost. The tour guides wore costumes. We saw an eighteenth-century French wedding. You and Jody danced with the wedding party."

"Yes!" cried Katie. "I was wearing the beautiful Ojibway mocassins my mom bought me."

"And do you remember how Kevin loved the musket and cannon demonstrations? You and Jody covered your ears. What a couple of sissies!" mocked the turtle.

"Your heart is as hard as your shell!" declared the mouse.

"Oh do be quiet, Jody! You're upsetting me. It was all beginning to come back to me," Katie complained.

"Your brother Kevin wanted to learn all about what the French and the Indians ate and drank in the 1700s," Jody reminded Katie. "I think the archaeologist at the fort told Kevin that the French imported ham, bacon, beef, and veal from Québec. I guess they drank cider wine and brandy."

"European brandy." Mich shook his head solemnly. "The innocent Indians killed off all their animals so they could sell the fur. They traded this fur for that bad European brandy and for red dye. The liquor made them drunk. The dye had lead in it. This lead poisoned many a warrior. It was so sad."

"What did the Indians eat? I forget." asked Katie.

"Oh they had orchards full of fruit. They also grew corn and beans," replied Mich. "They gathered blueberries and **tapped**, or drew off the syrup from the maple trees in the spring. They made the syrup into sugar. This sugar kept them alive through the cold winters. They also fished the Straits for trout, sturgeon, and whitefish. And they hunted elk, deer, and bear."

"Do you remember the Mighty Mackinac Bridge?" asked Mich.

"Oh yeah! It's the world's longest **suspension** (hanging) bridge. I guess it goes on for over four miles," said Katie.

"That's right! It's the best bridge ever. It **spans** (crosses) the five-mile wide strait between Mackinaw City and St. Ignace. It has 41,000 miles of wire in its main cables, which weigh 11,840 tons!" cried Mich with great enthusiasm.

My sister had fallen asleep. I found her snoring with Jody nestled in her arms. Mich the turtle was flipped over on his back on the floor.

Katie awoke to find the turtle wriggling on the floor.

"Help! Turn me over you great oaf of a girl!"

"Oh dear," she said, gently righting him again. "I certainly didn't mean to . . ."

"Never mind. Now where were we?"

"You were going on and on about the bridge." Jody complained.

"Never mind," Katie sighed. "I know what happened next. We boarded a hydro plane for Mackinac Island. It took 18 minutes to get there from Mackinaw City. I guess we had to leave our van on the mainland. But we took our bikes with us."

"I stood at the front of the boat, with you and your mother," Jody interrupted. "Just as the Grand Hotel came into view, the air began to be filled with the perfume of lilacs in full bloom." With this the mouse clapped his little paws together gleefully.

"I," said Mich, "was in the back of the ship with your father and brother. We watched the mainland vanish through the jet of water that fans out from the stern like a rooster tail.

"What can you guys tell me about the island itself? I can still see the water and the boats, the seagulls, the fudge, the horses, and carriages, but that's about all," said Katie sadly.

"All I remember is the fudge and the fort," said Jody. "I loved marching with my musket. And I'll certainly never forget how silly Mich here looked with fudge all over his face. Come to think of it, Mich is the expert. He was the one who acted as our guide during the whole trip. It's his home turf after all."

"Now that you mention it, that trip was sort of hard on me. First I was soaked in the Straits. After that I was dropped in fudge, and finally, I was thrown off Arch Rock," sulked the turtle. "I don't want to think about this any more. Why don't you ask Kevin to help you? He's the historian."

"Oh please, Mich. I don't want to ask that know-it-all for help."

"Sorry," said the turtle, folding his front legs across his chest. "I refuse to say another word. And that is that."

Katie had no choice but to ask me to help her write the rest of her story. Now I can tell it like it really was!

Our boat pulled up to a wooden dock. Heavy draft horses waited for supplies from the mainland to be taken off the boats and loaded onto their wagons.

I found out that there are 300 Percherons and Belgian Clydesdales on the island every summer. These strong work horses are bred at Amish Acres in Indiana. My sister loves horses. She rushed right up to a monster Percheron to pet it. She only came up to just above its knee.

"Come on, Katie. Grab your bike so we can explore this place!" said my dad, leading her away by the hand.

"No, ho, ho!" she began to cry.

"Here, you hold Mich," our mother told her. "Don't let him fall into the water again."

We pushed our bikes toward the town. We could see Fort Mackinac high up on the **bluff** (hill) overlooking the harbor.

On our left, at the water's edge, was the beautiful Victorian-style Iroquois Hotel. My mom wanted to eat lunch there because they have great food and a great view of the water. When I heard they served something called a "Mackinac Island Fudge Ice Cream Puff," I was hungry too.

They say Mackinac Island is a living Victorian Village. When we got onto Main Street, we saw the Windemere Hotel with its big front porch. My mom loves Victorian elegance.

"Let's go see the Grand Hotel first." she beamed. "It's the world's largest summer hotel, isn't it Mike? I guess it was built in 1887."

Our father consulted his guidebook. "Yes, Mary. According to this, it was built by railroad and steamship companies to encourage travel to the island. It has a 660-foot veranda, and a serpentine pool that's open to the public."

"Oh!" exclaimed our mother, "that's where Esther Williams swam when she starred in *This Time for Keeps* with Jimmy Durante."

"Who *are* those people?!" I asked her. She told me *Somewhere in Time* with Christopher Reeves was filmed here too, but she never said who Esther and Jimmy whats-their-names were.

Anyway, the Grand Hotel was grand. It was at the top of Cadotte Avenue. There was an elegant cab with a coachman in a top hat and red coat. The building had majestic white columns and bright yellow awnings. Katie and Jody rolled down the lawn where the lilac bushes were blooming.

Suddenly, in the middle of our visit to the Grand Hotel, Katie began to tug at our father's big hand. It seems that she and Mich couldn't wait to visit the fudge shops on Main Street.

Back in town, we peered in the windows of Ryba's, Murdick's, JoAnn's, and May's as the fudge makers poured the candy base from big copper kettles onto marble slabs. Katie persuaded us to go inside one of the shops to get a closer look. What a mistake!

We watched the candymaker knead the cooling fudge mixture with a wooden paddle to take out the air bubbles. This is what makes the fudge thick and heavy.

Mich was so overcome with emotion that he felt faint - according to Katie.

My sister says Mich cried out in Mac-Turtle - the language she claims he speaks. I never heard him utter a sound. But I did see him go *kerplop* onto the marble slab.

The candy maker looked upset as he fished the turtle out of his candy.

"Hey kid! You got fuzz from your doll in my fudge. Now I gotta mix up a whole new batch."

Our poor mother was ashamed. Holding Mich by his only clean leg, she apologized to the candy maker. Luckily he was a kind person. He didn't charge us for the candy Mich had ruined.

"Well it looks like Mich has had it," said my dad. "I think his time on this planet is up."

My sister began her wail with a series of "No, ho, ho's" that grew louder and louder as she stomped her foot. Huge tears began to trickle down her chubby cheeks.

"Well, Mike," said my mom to our father, "Maybe we should find our room and see if we can't save Mr. Turtle. What do you think?"

Our father heaved a deep sigh. We pushed our bikes up Main Street to Bogan Lane, where my parents had reservations.

My mom soaked and scrubbed Mich and hung him out to dry again. Then we took off for the Round Island Bar and Grill at Mission Point Resort. It was a great place to watch the freighters while we ate our dinner.

Our waiter told us the freighters headed West are loaded with iron ore from Minnesota. These boats pass through Lake Superior, the Soo (the boat locks at Sault Ste Marie), and upper Lake Huron. When they pass out of the Straits, they head for Lake Michigan, Chicago, and Gary, Indiana.

After dinner we walked along the shore. Big fog horns boomed. We even saw some bats. Cool!

The next morning, when we woke up, Katie's bed was empty. We looked everywhere, but my sister had vanished along with Mich and Jody.

"Don't worry, Mary," my dad said to my mom. "This island was made for kids to explore. I'm sure she's safe. I'll get dressed and look for her."

My mom wasn't so sure about that. She knew that if there was trouble to get into, Katie would find it.

My dad came back to the room frantic. Katie's bike was missing. My mom was sure Katie had drowned because of the disaster that had happened during our trip to Holland, Michigan. But that's another story.

"Where could she have gone?" my mother sniffed. "She's such a little thing - so helpless."

Something told me that "helpless little thing" was just being a brat.

No one wanted any breakfast. The hotel notified the island police for us. My dad and I

set out to find Katie on our bicycles. My mom stayed behind in case the police called.

My dad figured we should cover the shoreline first to make sure my sister hadn't fallen in the water. We raced around the outer edge of the island. That took us about an hour and fifteen minutes because it's only eight or nine miles.

I got glimpses of Devil's Kitchen, a small limestone cave, the British Landing, and Arch Rock, a huge arch made out of limestone. But there was no sign of Katie, Mich, or Katie's bike.

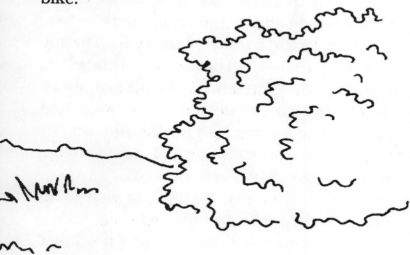

My stomach was knotted up. I was angry that Katie was spoiling this beautiful trip for me. I was also afraid we might never find her.

When dad and I got back to our hotel my mother was emotional. My dad decided to rent a couple of horses. If we hadn't been worried sick, it would have been like being in a movie.

When we arrived at the stable, we got our first clue to Katie's whereabouts. Her pink bicycle with the green tassles on the handlebars was leaning against a wall.

"That's her bike!" my dad cried.

How could you *not* know whose bike it was? I couldn't believe she chose those colors.

We looked all around the stable.The guy who ran the place told us that one of his horses was gone. He figured his assistant had rented it out. He hadn't noticed the bike. Katie had taken riding lessons with me the summer before, but she was still too small to get onto the horse by herself. We were puzzled.

"Don't let's say anything to your mom until we check this out," my dad said.

The police had lent my dad a cellular phone. He called them to let them know he thought Katie might be on horseback.

We must have combed every trail on the Island, looking for my sister and her stupid stuffed toys. We went past some really spectacular limestone rock formations. One of them is called Sugar Loaf. This limestone stack rises 75 feet above the ground. The Indians thought it was the Great Spirit's Great Wigwam.

From time to time, my dad called to see if my sister had been found and to try to cheer my poor mother up. I guess we were going in circles because we found ourselves back at Arch Rock. A carriage full of people had stopped with their tour guide.

The guide told us how the rock got a hole in it. According to legend, a young Indian girl was held prisoner at the top of the cliff by her father because he didn't want her to marry a young spirit prince. The girl cried so much her tears washed away the stone. That is how the Indians believe the arch was made.

The Indians also thought that Arch Rock was where the Great Spirit entered the island.

My dad and I peered down the steep cliff through the arch. Maybe we would see Katie walking or riding along the beach far below us.

As we leaned over the steep incline, we caught a glimpse of something round and fluffy in the brush, not too far down.

"Oh no!" cried my father." I think it's Mich."

I thought I heard tears in his voice. He gave me the reins to hold while he went after that sorry stuffed turtle.

Sure enough, my father returned with the turtle in tow and tears in his eyes. He was afraid Katie's horse had stumbled and thrown her over the cliff. He telephoned the police because he thought they should search the cliffside for my sister.

The police came in a car! My mom was with them. Her eyes were all swollen from crying. I couldn't believe this was happening. Someone took our horses back to the stable for us. The three of us just stood there staring helplessly over that cliff. I was numb. My mother was in agony.

An hour went by without any further progress. Then one of the officers got a call on his telephone. At first he knitted his brow. My heart churned. I was sure it was some bad news about my sister. Then the policeman's face broke into a broad grin.

"Mr. Murphy," he said, signaling to my dad to come closer, "I think we've located your daughter!"

"Is she . . ."

"She's just fine. Not a scratch on her. But she wants her turtle."

"Where is she?!" my father cried, his voice catching in his throat.

* * *

My sister had gone for a ride on "Walter" the horse. I guess Walter tired of his burden because he had tossed her onto the lawn at Fort Mackinac. Walter went home to his stable, leaving Katie to explore the fort. She struck up a conversation with a soldier there. He was the one who had called the police.

According to Katie, Mich the turtle had suggested an early morning ride. I found this hard to believe. But she insisted that he had led her and Jody to the stable. There they had found a ladder.

"We leaned it up against Walter's stall." she explained. "Mich held it, while Jody and I climbed up. Once we were all on top of the stall, Walter moved over so we could slide onto his back. Poor Mich. Where is he?"

Once my sister remembered Mich, she began to get tearful. The Police Chief brought the turtle from the car. Katie chattered to him excitedly in MacTurtle. She translated what she said so that I could write it into our story:

"Jody and I were so worried about you! You missed all the fun. Jody got to play soldier while you were lost," my sister told the turtle.

I was glad Katie had been found, but I was angry because she always managed to become the center of attention. What a drama queen! My parents got so emotional about my sister they didn't even notice me.

My parents tried to explain to Katie that she was lucky Walter the horse didn't throw her off Arch Rock. She covered her ears until my dad threatened her with a time out. Time out is a torture for my sister because it means she has to be quiet.

We ate lunch in the Harbor View Dining Room at the Chippewa Hotel. My mom wanted to go there because they serve great whitefish. There's also an awesome view.

During dinner we decided to walk up market Street toward Fort Street so we could take in some of the history of this place.

As we made our way to the historic home of Robert and Elizabeth Stuart, Katie kissed and hugged Mich. She talked to him in Mac-Turtle. It was embarrassing. My mother carried Jody.

Stuart house was big and white. It had been built out of wood during the early 1800s. Robert Stuart was the American Fur Company agent on the island. I guess the fur business was pretty profitable until the poor indians ran out of animals to kill for the French and British traders. The Indians did all the hunting. The fur companies got all the money.

Robert Stuart's house was pretty rad. I counted 25 windows on just the front of the building.

"This is me bored! This is me leaving!" Katie glared at me. She's such a pain. I'm really sorry I didn't get to count *all* the windows.

Next we saw McGulpin House - the oldest surviving building in Michigan. It was moved to the island from Michilimackinac in 1779 during the American Revolution. You could still see the original logs in some places.

Across the street from McGulpin House is a limestone building with wooden shutters, limestone chimneys, and **dormer windows** (upright windows in a slanting roof). This is the Beaumont Memorial building. It used to be the American Fur Company's retail store.

Alexis St. Martin was a French Canadian **voyageur** (canoe paddler). In 1822 he was shot in the stomach in the American Fur Company's store. It was an accident. Dr. Beaumont, from the fort, treated the wound.

The wounded man survived, but the hole in his stomach never closed up. Dr. Beaumont took him home with him so he could peer into that hole every day after Alexis ate. The doctor could watch how the man digested his food through that hole!

After a while, this Alexis got tired of being peered at and went away. Dr. Beaumont found him years later. He had taken a wife.

The doctor convinced Alexis to let him do more experiments. The canoe paddler only agreed to this because Dr. Beaumont promised to support his wife and children.

In 1833 Dr. Beaumont's famous *Experiments and Observations on the Gastric Juice and Physiology of Digestion* was published.

"See Katie!" I said to my sister. "Noticing things that seem unimportant or even dumb to other people can make a person famous."

"What? Like counting windows?" Katie snapped. "I don't think so."

The last place we had time to visit on Mackinac Island was the fort. I really enjoyed this place!

First of all, the soldiers there were like actors. They pretended to be the American men who actually lived there in the 1880s. It was as though they had stepped right out of history. Each man told us about his life at the fort, his family, and his military duties. He showed us how he played his fiddle or loaded his rifle.

We toured all the neat old buildings and learned about Indian, military, and home life in the late 19th century.

The French came to Mackinaw in 1671. They built Michilimackinac, the fort in Mackinaw City. The Indians liked the French because they had come here to trade for fur and do missionary work. Frenchmen married Indian women. The Indians taught the French how to hunt, fish, and garden.

The Indians fought side by side with the French against the British colonists. Unfortunately the French lost their forts to the British. They had to promise not to help the Indians win back their lands from the British.

The great Chief Pontiac was very angry. He united the tribes of the region and fought bravely against the British. He didn't know his French friends could no longer help him. When he found out they wouldn't come to his rescue, he retreated for the winter. The following spring, the tribes separated and went home.

The British were greedy and cruel. Commander Geoffrey Amherst was the first person ever to use germ warfare. He sent blankets infected with small pox to the Lenape and Odawa tribes, who were fighting with Chief Pontiac's tribe. Many Indians fell sick and died of small pox.

We took the last ferry back to the mainland that evening. The island was lit by a brilliant sunset on Lake Michigan. I felt sad. I wished we could have stayed longer. There was so much we didn't get to see. I'd really like to go back there someday - without Mich.

"Why did you have to write such mean things about Mich?" Katie demanded to know. It was a cold November night two years later. I had just read our story to her by the firelight.

"Because he's trouble," I answered, bitterly.

"None of what went on was his fault," said Katie, matter-of-factly. "Everything that happened was my idea."

She must be growing up! I thought to myself with hope in my heart.

"Isn't that so, Mich?" my sister asked the big stuffed green dummy in her lap. She addressed him in "Macturtle." This language sounds suspiciously like "Hollmouse," and "Frankencoon," if you listen closely.

THE END

Join the FUN

Get Your **FREE** Subscription to

Jody's Travel Quarterly[©]
a Newsletter for Kids

Call 1 888-ask JODY
1 888-275 5639